Vintage Pop-Up Cards

Vintage Pop-Up Cards

Making Your Own Timeless Treasures

by Taylor Hagerty

LARK BOOKS

A Division of Sterling Publishing Co., Inc.

New York

A Red Lips 4 Courage Communications, Inc. book
www.redlips4courage.com
Eileen Cannon Paulin, *President*
Catherine Risling, *Director of Editorial*

10 9 8 7 6 5 4 3 2 1

First Edition

Published by Lark Books, A Division of Sterling
Publishing Co., Inc.
387 Park Avenue South, New York, N.Y. 10016

Text © 2007, Taylor Hagerty
Photography © 2007, Lark Books
Illustrations © 2007, Lark Books

Distributed in Canada by Sterling Publishing,
c/o Canadian Manda Group, 165 Dufferin Street
Toronto, Ontario, Canada M6K 3H6

Distributed in the United Kingdom by
GMC Distribution Services,
Castle Place, 166 High Street, Lewes, East Sussex,
England BN7 1XU

Distributed in Australia by Capricorn Link (Australia)
Pty Ltd., P.O. Box 704, Windsor, NSW 2756 Australia

If you have questions or comments about this book,
please contact:
Lark Books
67 Broadway
Asheville, NC 28801
(828) 253-0467

Manufactured in China

ISBN 13: 978-1-60059-031-3
ISBN 10: 1-60059-031-4

For information about custom editions, special sales,
premium and corporate purchases, please contact
Sterling Special Sales Department at (800) 805-5489
or specialsales@sterlingpub.com.

Table of Contents

Introduction

Any collector of vintage pop-up cards will tell you, there is something about a pop-up card that offers an unmistakable charm. I spotted my first card many years ago while searching through a box of old ephemera. It was a valentine card that lay flat, until I pulled down the bottom piece, realizing it took on a completely different, dimensional shape. The heart popped up, as did the boy and girl holding each end. What a sweet sentiment, I thought, and thus my passion for pop-up cards was born.

My card collection has grown to include other dimensional cards. Some have tabs that can be pulled to reveal a special sentiment, or paper cutouts that move with the tug of a central paper attachment. Today my collection has grown to more than 200 cards, from floral displays and children to holiday-themed cards and valentines. Though many stand at 3"x5", I have some as large as 24".

A desire to share my cards, without depleting my collection, inspired me to copy and recreate some of my favorites. I've been able to retain the period charm of the cards while adding many embellishments to update them with today's sophistication.

In this book, I've hand picked 24 of my favorite cards and created dazzling card projects. The cards have already been disassembled, color copied, and reassembled, retaining as much of their original design as possible. Simply photocopy the paper elements, reassemble, and follow the step-by-step instructions to embellish and decorate to create your own dimensional card projects that truly are works of art.

History of Pop-Up Cards

The beginnings of pop-up greeting cards go back into antiquity. The development of wood block printing by the Chinese and Japanese origami in the early 900s set the stage for many "mechanical" devices in books and greeting cards. The advent of the printing press and later the postal system made making and sending greeting cards of all kinds much simpler and more affordable.

In 1860, Luther Meggendorfer was one of the first entrepreneurs to capitalize on the superior technical capabilities of the German printing industry. He produced movable picture books with unfolding panoramas and pop-ups containing intricate die cuts for moving mechanical parts, engineered to provide animated graphics.

Victorian ingenuity led to the development of other printed paper items, most notably greeting cards that became fanciful and ingenious, incorporating moving parts in the form of pullouts and pop-ups. Pop-up greeting cards and paper doll books were very popular and featured hand painting, writing, locks of hair, colored seals, and ribbons. In the 1840s, cobweb or beehive cards became popular. Innovations included "mechanical" or movable cards that contained doors or shutters that opened, or moving parts that could be riveted or attached by pull-tabs. Other apparatus included complicated hinges to support stand-up cards. Unlike a basic folded card with a message inside, these cards had a tassel or other embellishment attached to a spiral of paper, which, when lifted, revealed a message. Some were simple cards using paper springs to create a three-dimensional effect. More substantial cards created a real sense of depth when opened.

World War I brought this golden era to an end and it was several years before the publishing industry again regained the confidence to experiment with paper engineering. World War II presented another interruption in the development of the pop-up. Apart from paper-engineered greeting cards and relatively simple pop-up books, where the pictures pushed up without the need for glue-tabs, there was relatively little interest in the medium during the 1950s and early '60s.

In the 1980s paper-engineered cards enjoyed a rebirth as interest in Japanese origami grew in popularity and the art form crossed over from a simple greeting card to a gift. To date, the three-dimensional greeting card has become established in its own right, not only as a distinctive form for carrying graphics, but also as an economical gift possessing a charm that has intrigued people who send and collect cards.

All of the projects featured in this book have their beginnings as actual pre-1920s pop-up and dimensional cards. Generally cards that are this old are in very fragile condition and their adhesive is usually fairly brittle. Thus, the concept of this book. A gallery of cards has been carefully disassembled, embellished, and reassembled. The cards are shown in their original form and the pieces are provided with each card. With step-by-step instructions for constructing and updating with today's crafting materials, in no time at all you'll have a unique vintage pop-up card of your own.

Actual copies of vintage pop-up cards are provided, along with instructions for new assembly. Simply color copy and embellish to your heart's content to create your own timeless treasures.

Getting Started

All of the vintage pop-up cards featured throughout this book were carefully disassembled to retain as much of their original design as possible. We've provided a photograph of each card in its original state and the paper elements that compose each card, along with a photograph of the embellished project.

In this section, you'll discover how to photocopy and cut out paper elements for each of the projects. You'll also learn how to reassemble the cards with proper adhesives and paper tabs, reinforce the cards as necessary, and master the simple techniques to embellish your projects.

Also listed are many of the embellishments that will help make updating your vintage pop-up cards fun and achievable, from charms and ribbons to glitter and rhinestones.

If you are working with original cards, I've included a few tips and techniques for disassembling and reassembling your own cards, opening the door of possibilities for designing your own fanciful vintage pop-up projects.

Scan paper elements using a computer, scanner, and image-manipulation software. Check for color accuracy and adjust as needed to eliminate any unwanted yellow tones on faces and then print from a color printer. If you don't have the equipment to scan and print at home, take the images to a copy center and make a color photocopy, adjusting colors as necessary. Enlarging a small image makes it possible to use embellishments such as silk or paper flowers that match the scale of the image. If needed, make multiple copies for layering and stacking cutouts. For a firm card that can stand on its own, be sure to copy paper elements onto cardstock.

Aging Your Paper: Be sure to use acid-free scrapbook paper or cardstock (110 lb. works best) for all images as this will ensure that the card will last for many years. Use textured cardstock to imitate a canvas look that can be distressed with an emery board or fine-grit sandpaper for a faded, vintage appearance.

What You'll Need
- Cardstock
- Computer and printer
- Emery board or sandpaper
- Image-manipulation software
- Photocopier
- Scanner

A

B

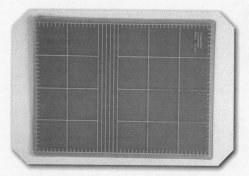

Using very sharp scissors, cut the image from the page, trimming as closely as possible to the edges of the image. Use detail or precision scissors or a craft knife for fine detail cuts. Try not to end a cut in a corner or on a dead end as doing so will leave unattractive cut marks. Wherever possible, cut in a continuous line by turning the paper instead of chopping the scissor blades. Leave difficult spots until

last and use a sharp craft knife to make the final cuts on a cutting mat. As you are cutting out the piece, periodically flip it over and check the back for ragged edges or cuts that don't meet. It is easier to see problems on the plain back than on the printed side. Pull the edges through to the back with the dull side of the knife blade and trim off the pieces. For large, straight pieces, use a paper trimmer.

C

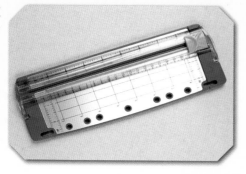

D

What You'll Need

- Craft knife (A)
- Cutting mat (B)
- Paper trimmer (C)
- Scissors: craft, precision/micro-tip (D)

Some pop-up cards become top or front heavy after they've been embellished. Create a simple easel to support the card so it can be properly displayed. The easiest support is created by simply folding a piece of cardstock in half and adhering it onto the back of the card, being careful that it doesn't show through any of the card's cutouts. Adjust the height and width of the easel card to compensate for different sizes of pop-ups. The easel can be used to add the recipient's name and date to the card.

✿ REINFORCING CARD WITH WIRE

Support top-heavy cards by reinforcing the backside using craft wire. Outline the back of the card shape in wire, bending as necessary to straighten the project, and secure with acid-free cellophane tape. A smaller gauge wire is useful for supporting smaller pop-up images that have trouble remaining upright within a card or by itself.

What You'll Need

- Acid-free cellophane tape
- Craft wire
- Needle-nose pliers
- Wire cutters

Diamond cut: A cut made in the fold of the card. It offers stronger support for items that come out further from the card.

Diorama: A scenic representation in which an image is seen from a distance through an opening. The scene can be composed of several layers to enhance the feeling of depth.

Spring: A circle of heavyweight paper cut into a spiral. Used to make an element "pop" from the background.

Tab: The most common method of adding dimension. The tab can be pulled to create movement or can be used as a support.

V-fold: Used in pop-ups that have several layers such as a scene. The layers are glued onto the card base in a "V" shape.

Volvelle: A paper disc in a book or card that, when rotated, can be used as a tool for calculations or other less scientific purposes, such as fortune telling. It is considered the first movable paper to appear in a book.

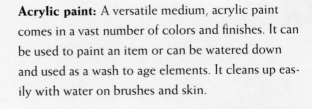

✿ EMBELLISHMENTS

Acrylic paint: A versatile medium, acrylic paint comes in a vast number of colors and finishes. It can be used to paint an item or can be watered down and used as a wash to age elements. It cleans up easily with water on brushes and skin.

Beads: Beads of all kinds, from tiny seed beads to ornate bugles to elegant pearls, add a sophisticated touch to a card. String them on wire as a dimensional accent. Applying beads directly onto paper requires beading glue or tacky double-sided tape for a strong bond.

Brads: Available in an array of colors, shapes, and sizes, some have loops for stringing ribbon or fibers through, similar to lacing a shoe. To use a brad, simply poke a small hole in the paper using a piercing tool, insert the brad, and flatten the prongs on the back of the paper.

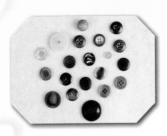

Buttons: Buttons add a dimensional element to any design. An almost limitless variety to choose from means you can find the right look for any project. Adhere buttons with glue dots, craft glue, a hot glue gun, or tacky double-sided tape.

Charms: These little ornaments add a pleasing dimensional touch to a card. Secure charms to the design using glue dots, foam dots, craft glue, or a hot glue gun.

Fabric and trims: Small bits of fabric, braid, ribbon, or trim add interest and dimension to a card. Many patterned fabrics can be photocopied to create custom papers for card designs. Adhere using fabric glue, glue dots, foam dots, craft glue, or a hot glue gun.

Glitter: There is a variety of glitter types in an enormous color palette available to embellish a card design. To ensure a solid bond, use tacky double-sided tape, glitter adhesive, or adhesive paper.

Paper: The primary element used in creating cards, paper is available in a variety of colors, types, weights, and textures. Types include cardstock, decorative (or scrapbook), hand-made, mulberry, and vellum. Paper can be adhered using practically any type of adhesive.

Paper doilies: Square, round, and heart-shaped paper doilies are valuable accents. Use them on the card itself or on the easel supporting the card. Designs in the doilies can be snipped and used as desired.

Rhinestones: Rhinestones add a rich sparkle to a design. Rhinestones with an adhesive backing are the easiest to use. Sequins are another great way to add a rich sparkle to a design. Adhere with glue dots, craft glue, or tacky double-sided tape.

Silk flowers: Made from ribbon or fabric, silk flowers give a lovely dimensional look to a card. Create leaves by cutting velvet ribbon scraps into leaf shapes and crushing them, then adhere them behind flowers. Use the same adhesives as those used with fabrics.

Adhering Rhinestones & Sequins: Roll a small ball of beeswax and attach it to the end of a toothpick. Place a small amount of beading or craft glue on a piece of cardboard. Pick up the rhinestone or sequin by pressing the beeswax onto the top of the stone or sequin. Dip the back lightly into the glue and wipe off the excess on the cardboard. Place as desired and then remove it from the toothpick by pressing lightly on the stone or sequin with your fingernail or craft tweezers.

Applying Glitter: With slight pressure, glide glitter adhesive bottle tip across the paper to get the thinnest, smoothest, least broken line of adhesive possible. Add more pressure to make different line widths. Using a spoon, sprinkle glitter onto the glue and then tap off the excess. It is important to apply the glitter to the glue while it is wet, white, and shiny, within 15–30 seconds.

Beading: A few lovely beads in coordinating colors strung on wire can embellish projects and add an interesting dimensional element to a card. Strips of tacky double-sided tape covered in seed beads make a beautiful border accent.

Chalking: Use chalks to easily age a paper element, create soft backgrounds, add shading to die cuts or stamped images, or highlight elements. Apply chalks using cosmetic sponges, cotton balls, or cotton swabs. This versatile medium can be used wet or dry. Dry chalks are very forgiving tools because they can be erased and reapplied as needed.

Fig. 1

Fig. 2

Fig. 3

Fig. 4

Fig. 5

Fig. 6

Creating Paper Pompoms: Adjust pompom size to fit project by increasing or decreasing sizes of punches. Our example uses cardstock. If a lighter weight paper is used, add additional layers of shapes to compensate for the thickness.

Materials
- Brad
- Cardstock
- Cosmetic sponge
- Glue dots
- Hole punch
- Inkpad: pigment
- Paper punches: flowers ranging from 1½" to 2" (2-3)

Instructions
1. Punch flowers of each size from cardstock. (Fig. 1)
2. Ink edges of each shape using inkpad and cosmetic sponge; allow to dry. *Note:* Be sure to lightly apply ink to the fronts of the shapes. (Fig. 2)
3. Pierce small hole in center of each shape using hole punch. (Fig. 3)
4. Bend or crumple each shape; smooth out. Layer pieces together with largest on bottom and smallest on top. (Fig. 4)
5. Thread brad through holes and flatten prongs on back of stack of shapes, securing layers together. (Fig. 5)
6. Separate and arrange layers, bending as needed to give added dimension. (Fig. 6)
7. Adhere pompom to project using one or more glue dots.

Circles Made Easy
Since the circle shapes don't have to be perfect, try cutting the shapes by hand or cutting a template and duplicating the circles. It's also fun to try different shapes and paper. Handmade paper looks like a fabric flower and using different colors adds dimension. Use colored tissue paper to make fluffy pompoms.

Disassembling Pop-Up Cards

You may decide to use the techniques and ideas in this book to work with your own original. To disassemble a card, begin by examining it closely. There are probably one or more places where the papers have begun to lift. Start with an area that is relatively loose and begin to very carefully detach the papers. Use a razor blade or craft knife to separate areas that are more firmly attached. If you reach a point where it is necessary to actually cut or tear apart pieces, try to work from the backside to disguise any damage and preserve the printed image. Use acid-free cellophane tape to reinforce the back of weak areas.

For particularly stubborn areas, you may need to steam the card. Bring a pot of water to a full boil and hold the card in the steam. Do not hold the card too closely to the pot so that you do not touch the water or oversaturate the card. Hold the card in the steam for a few moments and then check to see if the adhesive has loosened. Repeat the process until the pieces come apart and then allow the card to dry.

Assembling Cards

A traditional pop-up card becomes dimensional through the use of different mechanisms. When closed, the card lies flat and can be easily stored and mailed (A). When the card stands up (B) the elements move forward by use of paper hinges or tabs. This is generally a piece of paper on the bottom of an image that is folded and adhered onto a base or background (C). A hinge can also be used on the back of an element. A pull-tab is used to create motion in a display. It is a long strip of cardstock that has an image on one end (D). Two slits are made in the

A

B

C

D

E
F
G

back of the card base; the end of the pull-tab is threaded through the back of the pop-up and out through the front (E). The pull-tab is folded and adhered to itself to create the "pop-up" dimension (F). When the tab is pulled or slid from side to side, the image on the opposite end moves.

If you want to embellish your card and it is not necessary that the card lies flat, cut a small tab, about ½"x2", from cardstock and adhere to each paper element. Then attach the elements to your card base, referring to the project image provided

H

for placement. You can use the tabs from an original card (G) or cut and add your own. Replicate the pop-up's dimensional appearance (H) by stacking adhesive foam dots behind individual images. One or two layers of dots are subtle while four or more will push out the element quite far and will be very noticeable. Using several stacks of foam dots is a good way to support a particularly heavy element. It is very helpful to photograph the card in its original state, both expanded and flat, as well as from the sides before and during the process of disassembling the card. When you reassemble it, you will be able to refer to the pictures to be sure you are putting it back together correctly.

Remember, though, if you don't plan on folding your card shut, there's no need to create pull tabs that allow the card to open and close.

March the 1858

Emma L. Ritchie

Remember me when far away

If only he

Card Projects

Put on Your Thinking Cap

Ideal for a special graduate or favorite teacher, Put on Your Thinking Cap contains vintage academic touches that hearken back to primary school days. This project uses an elevated paper base of penmanship paper or, for a simpler design, the pop-up portion of the card can be removed from the base.

Original Card

✿ ADHESIVES

- Clear-drying craft glue
- Glitter adhesive
- Glue dots
- Mini foam dot
- Tacky double-sided tape

✿ MATERIALS

- Brad: pewter mini star
- Cardstock: black
- Glitter: ultra-fine black, gold, hunter green, red
- Paper elements: cap, diploma, quotation, ruler tape, school report card
- Vellum butterfly wings

✿ TOOLS

- Computer and printer
- Copier
- Craft knife
- Cutting mat
- Fine tips (for glue bottles)
- Pencil
- Ruler
- Scissors: craft, micro-tip, pinking shears
- Stapler and staples

PUT ON YOUR **THINKING** CAP

congratulations sarah.

chool for the Term

(Year.)

✿ INSTRUCTIONS

1 Copy and cut out paper elements (page 25). Using craft knife, cut out small areas in background.

2 Using glitter adhesive, embellish paper elements with glitter: hunter green on dress folds; red glitter on flowers; gold glitter to create small dots on flowers; and black glitter to create dots on vellum wings. *Note:* Let each color dry before applying the next color.

3 To create paper base: Cut 12"x2½" strip (for stand) and 2"x5" piece of black cardstock (for lid). Cut 12"x2" piece of school report card paper with pinking shears. Cut 3" length of ruler tape paper. Glue school report card paper to stand strip, centering it so borders are even. Staple strip into circle shape. With staples at front right side, press down on loop to flatten. Pinch in sides about ½" on either side of fold to make vertical pleats. Fold a few times to remove some of spring in loop. Using glue dots rolled into balls, adhere lid to stand. Cover staples with strip of ruler tape paper and glue ends inside box. Trim excess ruler tape paper.

The paper sentiment at top is secured with a star brad and echoes the card's theme.

4 To embellish girl: Adhere glittered wings to back of girl (A) using glue dots. Adhere cap and diploma with glue dots. Print sentiment on paper; curl quote strip to give it a waving appearance and adhere to top of base with brad. Print out "Congratulations" sentiment and adhere with mini foam dot.

5 Attach girl to background (C) with paper tab (B) and glue dots. Glue piece to paper base.

Altering the Theme

Transform this graduation card into a birthday greeting with a party hat and noisemaker, or make a bride with a veil and bouquet and embellish the flowers with pastel glitter for a special wedding card.

A

B

C

The Garden Gate

From the gold-embossed gate to the glittering flowers, The Garden Gate is a treat for the senses, including the sense of smell. Applying rose essential oil to the silk rose petals, if desired, is a perfect way to send sweet "scent-iments" to someone special.

'Tis just a little Valentine
to prove my heart is true
I hope that you will think of me
Because I think of you

Original Card

✿ ADHESIVES

- Clear-drying craft glue
- Glitter adhesive
- Repositionable adhesive
- Tacky double-sided tape

✿ MATERIALS

- Cardstock: light pink (to match color on printed fence)
- Embossing adhesive
- Embossing inkpad: clear
- Embossing powder: gold
- Flowers: small rosebuds
- Glitter: ultra-fine gold, hot pink, light blue, light pink, pale green, pale yellow, periwinkle blue

✿ TOOLS

- Border punch
- Copier
- Craft knife
- Cutting mat
- Heat tool
- Paintbrush
- Pencil
- Ruler
- Scissors: craft, micro-tip
- Scoring tool

"'Tis just a little Valentine
To prove my heart is true
I hope that you will think of me
Because I think of you

Larks
EXTRA MILD

✿ INSTRUCTIONS

1 Copy and cut out paper elements (page 29). Using craft knife, cut out small areas in background. *Note:* Do not cut out the pink paper in the spaces between the fence rails.

2 To prepare base: Cut pink cardstock to 7"x6". Trim two long edges with border punch. Leave other two borders plain; set aside.

3 With paintbrush, apply ink from inkpad to gold fence rail (A); sprinkle with embossing powder and then apply heat tool to emboss. Flatten fence as it cools to keep it from curling.

4 To make easels for backs of all four strips: Trace around paper strips (B-D) on pink paper, making a rough silhouette and leaving enough at bottom to create ¼" flap. Glue silhouette to back of strip. No pink should peek out the front; trim it if it does. Fold this flap to make strip stand when adhered to base. *Note:* Do not permanently attach these yet.

5 To glitter remaining three panels: Using glitter adhesive and glitter, embellish roses with hot pink, light pink, and yellow glitter; dots on leaves with green glitter; white flowers with green glitter; and flowers with blue glitter, taking care to cover only bits of the flowers rather than entire flower; allow to dry. Add a few tiny rosebuds to create dimension.

6 To build the garden: Apply repositionable adhesive to bottom of each strip's flap and adhere each flap about 1" apart on pink paper base. Leave about 1" of space in front and in back of garden. Order of strips: gate (A), then cherub (B), then piece with green lawn in the middle (D), and finally, the three flowerpots (C). Once spacing is finalized, use double-sided tape over temporary adhesive to permanently adhere four garden strips to pink base.

Customizing the Sentiment

Customize the sentiment on the gate for all sorts of occasions. This project works beautifully as a Mother's Day, birthday, get well, or wedding card. Cover the existing sign's text with plain coordinating paper and glue dots. Create the greeting on coordinating cardstock and adhere on top of the covered sign with a foam dot for a dimensional effect.

28

A

'Tis just a little Valentine
To prove my heart is true
I hope that you will think of me
Because I think of you

B

C

D

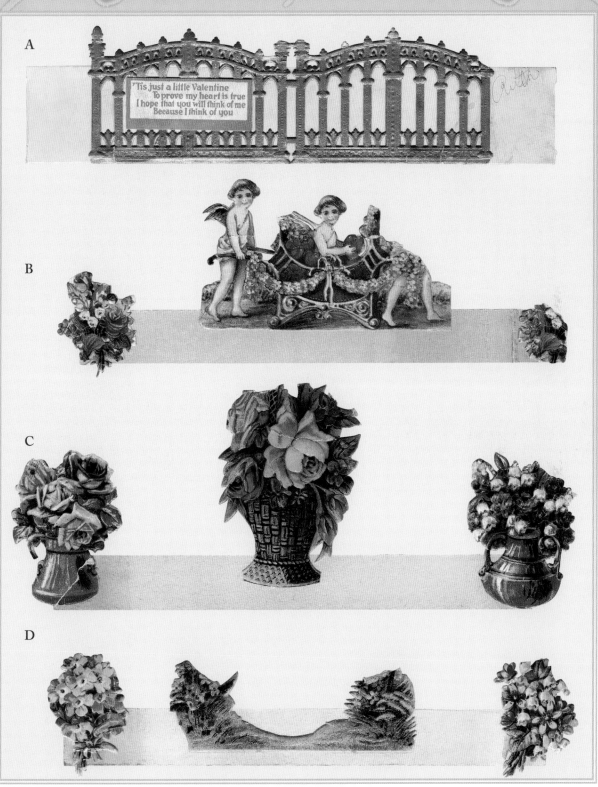

enlarge 125%

The Lily Harp

A true romantic, The Lily Harp card features hand painting, strips of old sheet music, and a velvet bow. The pearlized lilies of the valley and the brushstrokes of acrylic paint highlighted with glitter add substance and shine to a lovely card. A matte sealer keeps all of the new elements in place.

Original Card

✿ ADHESIVES

- Clear-drying craft glue
- Foam dots
- Glue dots
- Matte sealer
- Tacky double-sided tape

✿ MATERIALS

- Acrylic paint: shades of burgundy, green, and pink; white
- Craft wire (optional)
- Glitter: ultra-fine clear, dark red, green, pearl white, pink
- Matte sealer
- Old sheet music
- Ribbon: 1/8 " pink velvet
- Silk flowers: lilies of the valley, roses

✿ TOOLS

- Copier
- Craft knife
- Cutting mat
- Paintbrush
- Pencil
- Ruler
- Scissors: craft, micro-tip
- Wire cutters (optional)

✿ INSTRUCTIONS

1 Copy and cut out paper elements (page 33) twice. Using craft knife, cut out small areas in background.

2 Paint paper pieces (A, C) with light flourishes of paint to match colors: paint leaves with a brush or two of green shades; flowers with white, pinks, and burgundies; and ribbon bow with pinks. When dry, seal with light brushstrokes of matte sealer, then sprinkle with coordinating glitter colors. *Note:* Copiers vary and some inks may run so be sure to pre-test on scraps of printed images. Even if they blur a little the effect can be charming, especially when layered with clear and light-colored ultra-fine glitter. Do not soak images in paint.

3 Cut individual lily of the valley flowers from stems. Paint white, then sprinkle with pearl white glitter. Layer these several times for desired effect. When dry, glue to card.

4 Repeat Step 3 using roses and pink and red glitter.

5 To build the card: Attach each section with paper tabs (B). *Note:* The Lily Harp card shows the panels placed in an order different from the original so that the harp shows better. Hide any paper marks near the heart on the front of the harp with an extra floral strip adhered with foam dots.

Stacking several foam dots creates a strong support for pop-up layers.

6 To support the back of the card: Wire can be taped onto the back of the two biggest sections to support the weight of the panels, or, add a paper easel to the back by folding a piece of cardstock to 2"x3" and gluing or taping it to the back for added stability. *Note:* Wire should not be seen through the front cutouts.

7 Cut sheet music to 1½"x 24". Wrap sheet music around pencil to curl and then drape curled strip around card panels; trim ends as needed. Adhere with glue dots. Cut ribbon to 10", tie into bow, and glue to card.

Layering the Background
Stack foam dots four or five high and attach the flower layer to the background. This replaces the traditional paper tab behind some layers without adding much bulk.

A

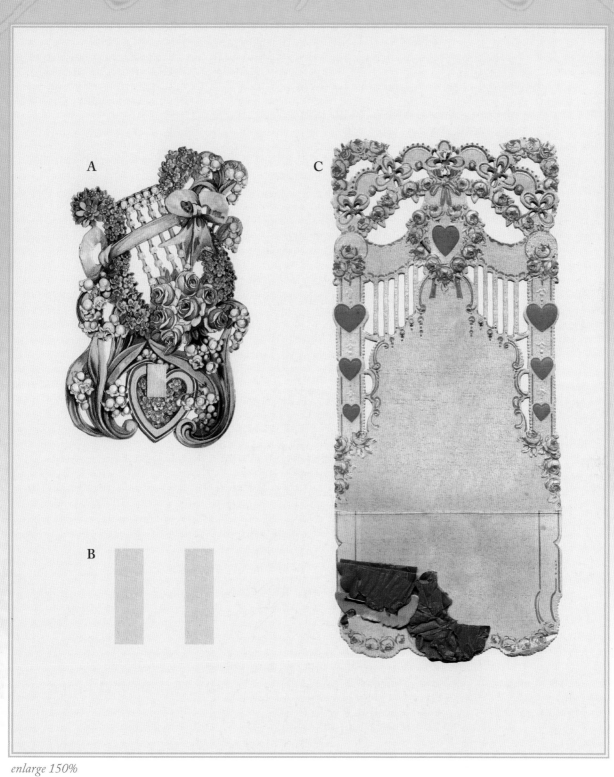

B

C

enlarge 150%

Token of Love

An unusual pop-up card, Token of Love hangs from a ribbon, allowing the four-leaf clover to fall open and display the greeting. The pansies and clover leaves are embellished with multiple colors of glitter and feature a dictionary definition containing the dual meaning of "pansy."

Original Card

✿ ADHESIVES

- Clear-drying craft glue
- Fabric glue
- Foam dots
- Glitter adhesive
- Glue dots
- Repositionable adhesive
- Tacky double-sided tape

✿ MATERIALS

- Cardstock: green
- Dictionary page
- Glitter: ultra-fine clear; golds, purples, and yellows (3 shades each)
- Lace or trim: ¼" white, about ½ yard
- Paper: beige
- Ribbon: ¼" silk, ½" green velvet

✿ TOOLS

- Copier
- Craft knife
- Cutting mat
- Fine tips (for glue bottles)
- Pencil
- Ruler
- Scissors: craft, fabric, micro-tip

hearts·ease (härts′ēz′) n. 1. Freedom from sorrow or care. 2. The pansy or various similar plants of the genus *Viola*. 3. The common persicaria, a plant. Also heart's′-ease′.

A TOKEN OF LOVE

1 Copy and cut out paper element three times (page 37). Cut around outside of one image and its reverse side and glue front to back so card is two-sided. Fold clover so verse faces out.

2 With third copy, cut out individual flowers and leaves (to be used for layering).

3 Using glitter adhesive, embellish separately cut pansy petals in shade of glitter to match. Use fine lines of glue as well as smeared patches. Cover edges of clover and background base around outer edges with gold glitter. *Note:* There's no need to glitter the centers; they will eventually be covered.

4 On light-colored pansies, cover petals with glittered cutout petals using foam dots. Using glue dots, adhere darker flowers. Cut freehand oval leaf shapes from ½" ribbon about 1"–2" long. Crumple, unfold, and tuck in between flowers as leaves with tips pointing out from pansies. Adhere with fabric glue.

5 To attach flower valentine to card: Cut two 4"x5" pieces of green cardstock and ½ yard of ¼" ribbon. Sandwich ribbon between cardstock so that loop is created at top. Using tacky double-sided tape, adhere two pieces of cardstock together, and then glue to back of card.

A photocopy of a dictionary definition adds an explanation to the general sentiment.

6 Glue white lace or desired trim around border of cardstock.

7 On copier, enlarge definition 160% or more, depending on size of original, and copy onto beige paper; adhere to front of card with foam dot. *Note:* You may need to trim size of foam dot so it is not visible behind definition.

Displaying Baseless Cards
Display pop-up cards that have no base on a hanging card base strung with a loop of ribbon or fanciful trim.

TOKEN OF

LOVE

enlarge 125%

Cupid in the Flowers

Cupid in the Flowers demonstrates a simpler version of cutting. Images are shaped into a general silhouette rather than trimmed in and around each flower. The design is embellished with glitter, a flower bead, and gold charms for added dimension.

✿ ADHESIVES

- Acid-free adhesive dispenser
- Glitter adhesive
- Glue dots
- Repositionable tape (optional)
- Tacky double-sided tape

✿ MATERIALS

- Bead: flower with rhinestone center
- Charms: small arrow, small heart
- Glitter: ultra-fine shades of blue, gold, and pink
- Leafing pen: gold
- Ribbon: ½" cream satin

✿ TOOLS

- Copier
- Craft knife
- Cutting mat
- Fine tip (for glue bottle)
- Scissors: craft, micro-tip

☆ INSTRUCTIONS

1 Copy and cut out paper elements (page 41). Using craft knife, cut out small areas in background.

2 With acid-free adhesive dispenser, adhere bottom element (E) to underside of base (G).

3 Paint edges of all paper elements with thin line of gold leafing pen; allow to dry.

4 Apply glitter adhesive where desired and sprinkle on glitter; allow to dry.

5 Attach smaller paper elements (A–D) to base (G) using paper tabs (F) and double-sided tape. If desired, use repositionable tape first to work out the spacing and placement of paper elements, and then secure with double-sided tape.

6 Attach charms, flower, cream ribbon, and desired sentiment with glue dots.

The paper elements are adhered to the base using tabs, just like in the original construction.

Cutting Simplified
Many pop-ups have intricate details that require precise cuts. Make a simpler version by cutting a general outline around each element. The white space left around the border can be left as is or colored using chalks or a leafing pen.

A

B

C

D

E

F

G

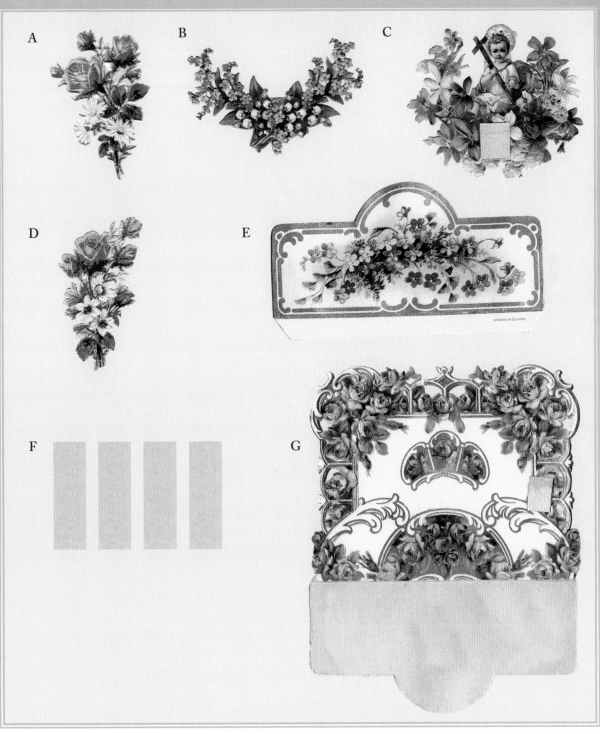

enlarge 115%

Most Beautiful Baby

The vintage-style honeycomb pedestal and the cherubic faces of the children on the Most Beautiful Baby card make it a lovely center-piece for a baby shower. Remove the honeycomb base and the pop-up can stand alone with back support as a sweet card for the new family.

Original Card

✿ ADHESIVES

- Clear-drying craft glue
- Foam dot
- Glitter adhesive
- Glue dots
- Hot glue gun and glue sticks

✿ MATERIALS

- Beads: blue crystal flowers (8-10)
- Craft wire
- Crystal teardrops
- Doilies: silver (2)
- Glitter: ultra-fine blues, deep rose, greens, silver
- Honeycomb ball: blue
- Paper flowers: small blue (10-20)

✿ TOOLS

- Copier
- Craft knife
- Craft wire
- Cutting mat
- Fine tips (for glue bottles)
- Micro-tip scissors
- Needle-nose pliers
- Wire cutters

✿ INSTRUCTIONS

1   Copy and cut out paper elements (page 45); repeat to create two sets of the bird for layering. Using craft knife, cut out small areas in background.

2   Apply glitter adhesive where desired and sprinkle on glitter; allow to dry between colors.

3   Apply small amount of glitter adhesive to half of paper flowers and sprinkle on blue glitter; allow to dry.

4   Attach flower crystal beads with bits of glue dots to grass area.

5   Attach paper flowers and glittered flowers, clustered at top, with glue dots. Hang crystals from top of card with craft wire using needle-nose pliers.

6   Adhere second bird to first bird with foam dot. Add paper element (A) to card base (C) with tabs (B).

7   To make base: Embellish edges of honeycomb with silver glitter. Glue to doily; allow to dry.

Two silver lace doilies finish off the base of the honeycomb with a subtle gleam.

8   Adhere card to top of honeycomb base with small amount of hot glue.

9   Wire back of card for support as necessary.

A

B

C

Merci!

Vintage ribbon beautifully dresses up the Merci! card. A color photocopy of an old wallpaper sample was used to create a backdrop that acts as an easel for the pop-up. Braided trims cover the base and the bulletin board card. The poodle has a pompom tail, fiber ears, and a textured body of glitter and paint.

Original Card

✿ ADHESIVES

- Acid-free adhesive dispenser
- Clear-drying craft glue
- Fabric glue
- Glitter adhesive

✿ MATERIALS

- Acrylic paint: pearl white
- Braids and fibers
- Cardstock: cream
- Decorative paper: copies of wallpaper and vintage mail
- Glitter: ultra-fine dark blue, green, light blue, rose, white
- Jewels
- Pompoms: white (2)
- Rhinestones: blue, dark pink, green
- Ribbon
- Spiral paper clip (optional)

✿ TOOLS

- Computer and printer
- Copier
- Craft knife
- Cutting mat
- Fine tips (for glue bottles)
- Paintbrush
- Pencil
- Ruler
- Scallop punch: oval
- Scissors: craft, micro-tip
- Scoring tool

❀ INSTRUCTIONS

1 Copy and cut out paper elements (page 49). Using craft knife, cut out small areas in background.

2 Adhere bottom element (A) to underside of base (D) using acid-free adhesive. Glue rhinestones onto flower basket on base (D).

3 Apply glitter adhesive and embellish with glitter: dark blue and light blue on flowers; rose on hat and clothing; and green in and around rhinestones in basket; allow to dry between colors.

4 Apply pearl white paint to poodle. With white glitter and paint, build up 3-4 layers to make hills, and 2-3 layers for valley. Tear one pompom in half. Glue torn pompom to dog's ear and whole pompom to tail.

5 Apply pearl white paint to birds; allow to dry. Apply glitter adhesive then sprinkle on white glitter.

6 Add rows of braid and trim around bottom of base (D), stopping to insert glittered and painted bird piece (B) with tab (C). Conceal base with layers of ribbon, wrapping ends around backside and securing with fabric glue.

7 To create the background: Cut and fold cardstock to create 5"x6" side-fold card using scoring tool. *Note:* The open card acts as an easel. With acid-

The side-fold card functions both as a place to write a note and as a support for the pop-up.

free adhesive dispenser, cover front of card with decorative paper. Add two strips of ribbon, making an "X"; tuck ends in back.

8 Print "Merci" in French script font and punch out with small oval punch; tuck into card front. If desired, add copy of old letter to background with spiral paper clip.

Embellishing Other Projects

Images can be printed and used outside the traditional pop-up format. Use a cutout of a basket of roses as a gift tag or a note card. You can also bind the side of an image and turn it into a miniature book or party invitation.

A

To my
Valentine.

D

B

C

enlarge 110%

Sew and Mend

Original Card

The Sew and Mend card uses color photocopies of treasured vintage-style embroidered linens to support the hand-sewn theme of the card. The pop-up girls stand on a flat, top-fold card that features a sewing needle packet embellished with a silver needle threader, buttons, and silk rosebuds.

✿ ADHESIVES

- Acid-free adhesive dispenser
- Clear-drying craft glue
- Glitter adhesive
- Hot glue gun and glue sticks

✿ MATERIALS

- Buttons: crystal (3)
- Canvas paper
- Cardstock: pale pink
- Copy of old stitchery
- Decorative paper
- Glitter: chunky teal; transparent hunter green, multi-color; ultra-fine deep rose, silver
- Needle card
- Needle threader
- Pearl-topped pin
- Silk flowers: roses (2); rosebuds (8)
- Trim: 1"-wide quilted trim (about 1 yard)

✿ TOOLS

- Copier
- Craft knife
- Cutting mat
- Fine tips (for glue bottles)
- Needle-nose pliers
- Pencil
- Ruler
- Scissors: craft scissors, micro-tip
- Scoring tool

1 Copy and cut out paper elements (page 53). Using craft knife, cut out small areas in background.

2 Using fine lines of glitter adhesive and glitter, embellish girls' clothing (A) to match. Glitter leaves and flowers, drying between colors.

3 Add very thin lines of glitter adhesive to edges of roses; sprinkle on rose-colored glitter and allow to dry.

4 With hot glue gun, attach rosebuds to front of girls (A) and rose to lower front spray of blue hydrangeas. Glue on glittered rose, without stem, on floor of card.

5 To assemble pop-up card: Glue paper tab (C) to hydrangea (B) and attach to base (D). Attach girl paper element (A) to base (D) with paper tabs (C).

6 To assemble sewing card: Cut and fold cardstock to create 8"x6" top-fold card using scoring tool. Using acid-free adhesive dispenser, adhere stitchery to front of card. Adhere 1" border of decorative paper along bottom of card and ad-

Adding packets of embroidery and sewing needles turns the pop-up card into a gift.

here quilted trim around edges. Glue buttons to corners, except for top right corner.

7 Glue remaining roses to top left of card. Embellish needle threader with silver glitter and glue to card. Add pearl-topped pin.

8 Glue pop-up card to top right corner of sewing card. If desired, add wording and sewing elements inside card.

Adding Family Heirlooms

Make unique papers that tell a family story using a color photocopy or color print of the scanned item. Do a practice run using a black-and-white copy to check for placement and sizing. Once the image is formatted correctly, print a color copy onto cardstock or fabric paper such as canvas or silk. This is a good way to incorporate an irreplaceable or bulky item such as a hankie or piece of lace.

A

D

B

C

Germany

To my Valentine

enlarge 115%

My Heart is Warm

Original Card

My Heart is Warm employs intricate cutting, a sentiment borrowed from another valentine, a silver heart charm, and a miniature thermometer to tie in the verse with the card. It was necessary to alter the pop-up a bit by cutting down some excess foliage in front of the girl's face.

✿ ADHESIVES

- Clear-drying craft glue
- Foam dots
- Glitter adhesive

✿ MATERIALS

- Beaded flowers
- Charm: heart
- Craft thermometer
- Glitter: ultra-fine dark blue, light blue, red, silver
- Leafing pen: silver

✿ TOOLS

- Copier
- Craft knife and extra blades
- Cutting mat
- Fine tips (for glue bottles)
- Micro-tip scissors
- Needle-nose pliers
- Scoring tool

✿ INSTRUCTIONS

1 Copy and cut out paper elements (page 57). Copy sentiment paper element (C) of Sunbeam Boy card (page 65). Using craft knife, cut out small areas in background.

2 Paint all edges with leafing pen to eliminate white. *Note:* For complete coverage, paint from backside as well.

3 With tiny amounts of glitter adhesive, embellish front of card with matching glitter colors.

4 Cut paper element (A) into three separate pieces, blue flowers at left and red flowers at right.

5 Glue on beaded flowers and add cluster in front to hide red honeycomb marks from original card. With glitter adhesive, embellish sentiment from Sunbeam Boy card with dark and light blue glitter; glue on craft thermometer.

6 To assemble card: Fold base (D) at bottom third of card using scoring tool. Using paper tabs

Simple paper tabs support the pop-ups.

(E), glue on heart paper element (C) first, and then children paper element (B) and foliage (A), which has been cut into three separate pieces. Adhere glittered verse to bottom right and heart charm at top of card with foam dots.

Keeping Tools Sharp

Invest in a pair of sharp precision or micro-tip scissors dedicated strictly to making detailed cuts on paper. Do not be tempted to use them to cut ribbon, fibers, or other paper as doing so will dull the blades and make the fine details much more difficult to execute. Whatever tool you choose to use, be sure the blades are sharp and replace or sharpen frequently.

A

B

C

D

E

enlarge 200%

Happily Ever After

The Happily Ever After card features painted flower blooms crusted with pigment powder and pearl glitter. Pearl accents are applied to individual flowers in the design and narrow blue silk ribbon is threaded through the cutout portions of the background. Due to the weight of the embellishments, the back of the card is reinforced with wire.

Original Card

✿ ADHESIVES

- Acid-free adhesive dispenser
- Clear-drying craft glue
- Fabric glue
- Foam dots
- Glitter adhesive
- Glue dot

✿ MATERIALS

- Acrylic paint: white
- Clear sealer
- Craft wire
- Glitter: ultra-fine deep pink, pearl white
- Paper: white
- Pearls
- Pigment powder: pearl white
- Rhinestone: blue
- Ribbon: blue silk
- Rubber stamp: sentiment
- Silk flowers: lilies of the valley (20)
- Stone: coral heart
- Trim: blue silk

✿ TOOLS

- Computer and printer
- Copier
- Craft knife
- Cutting mat
- Fine tips (for glue bottles)
- Paintbrush
- Pencil
- Scissors: craft, fabric, micro-tip
- Wire cutters (optional)

✿ INSTRUCTIONS

1. Copy and cut out paper elements (page 61), copying two sets of shaking hands. Using craft knife, cut out small areas in background (A).

2. Adhere back of base (C) to base (D) with acid-free adhesive dispenser.

3. Using fabric glue, adhere blue silk trim to base paper element (D), outlining edge.

4. Remove stems and leaves of silk flowers and then paint white; allow to dry. Brush flowers with thin coat of clear sealer. While still tacky, sprinkle with pigment powder; rub in with paintbrush. Repeat to achieve 3-4 coats of layers, drying between coats. Glue individual silk flowers on top of flowers on paper element (A); allow to dry.

5. Using glitter adhesive, embellish sash on girl paper element (B) with deep pink glitter and gloves with pearl white glitter.

6. Thread ribbon through holes of backdrop (A), ending with both tails at the bottom. Glue on pearls with fabric glue; allow to dry flat. Glue coral heart on top.

7. Cut small piece of foam dot and adhere to reverse side, center, of extra hand piece. Remove remaining backing paper and adhere hand piece to hands on pop-up card. Secure at left and right sides with small piece of rolled-up glue dot. *Note:* It should look a little bowed out but not so much that the back image of the hands shows in the wrong places.

8. Print out sentiment on white paper to create title banner; trim ends into a "V" cut. Stamp sentiment with craft glue then add pigment powder; allow to dry. Curl with pencil to give it a wave. Glue blue rhinestone onto left side of banner.

9. To assemble card: Add girl (B), then backdrop (A) with paper tabs (E). Adhere waving banner with stacked foam dots along base in front of kneeling girl. Reinforce backdrop with wire, as necessary.

Identifying Fonts

It is difficult to gauge how a computer font will print in color. To make choosing easier, print a master list of fonts and color choices. Type the name of the font and the first three or four letters of the alphabet in upper and lower case. Copy and paste several times and then go back and change each line of text to a different color. Print the document and save in a binder for reference.

A

C

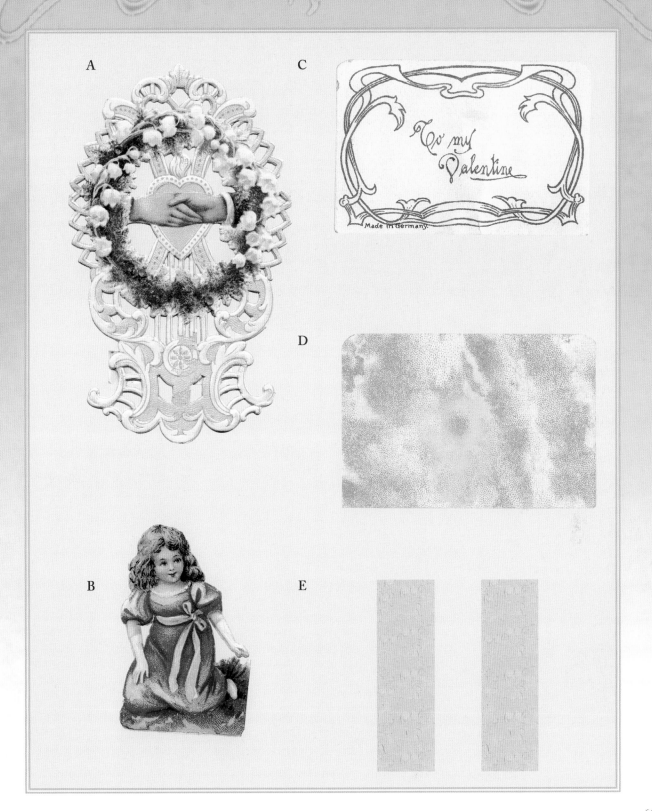

To my
Valentine

Made in Germany.

D

B

E

61

Sunbeam Boy

Original Card

A detailed openwork trellis is the backdrop to this stand-alone version of the Sunbeam Boy pop-up, which was reconstructed much like the original but with elaborate touches of glitter. The backdrop is edged with beads of glue and glitter to resemble tiny jewels. A paper honeycomb was trimmed and used to embellish the card base.

✿ ADHESIVES

- Acid-free adhesive dispenser
- Clear-drying craft glue
- Foam dots
- Glitter adhesive
- Glue dots

✿ MATERIALS

- Cardstock: desired color
- Craft wire (optional)
- Glitter: ultra-fine clear, gold, light teal, pearl, teal blue, white
- Honeycomb: pink
- Pigment powder: pearl white

✿ TOOLS

- Copier
- Craft knife
- Cutting mat
- Fine tips (for glue bottles)
- Paintbrush
- Scissors: craft, micro-tip
- Scoring tool
- Wire cutters (optional)

✿ INSTRUCTIONS

1 Copy and cut out paper elements (page 65), copying three sets of birds (A) for layering. Using craft knife, cut out small areas in background. *Note:* Take extra care cutting around trellis.

2 Adhere bottom of card base (B) to lower third of back side of card base (F) using acid-free adhesive dispenser.

3 Brush birds with pigment powder; allow to dry. Using glitter adhesive, embellish with glitter: birds with clear, light teal, pearl, and white; tiny flowers with light teal and teal blue glitter; and small amount of gold on boy's hair. Layer birds with stacks of three foam dots.

4 To assemble card: Fold lower third of card base using scoring tool. Using paper tabs (D), adhere boy (A) to back of card, then birds (E) at forefront. Adhere honeycomb to front, between bottom birds, with glue dots. *Note:* Be careful not to trim away too much honeycomb from party centerpiece. Adhere sentiment (C) to back of base (F) with glue dots.

5 Using fine tip, add border of craft glue in shape of small dots to look like beads. Sprinkle dots with

The paper easel functions both as a place to write a note and as a support for the pop-up.

pearl and clear glitter. Add wire backing to support card, if desired.

6 Add paper easel to back of card by folding piece of cardstock and gluing it in place.

Mailing Cards
If you'll be mailing a completed pop-up card, be sure to package it securely so it will arrive in showcase shape. Use padded mailing envelopes, which are available in several sizes. If the card is too big, package it in a box. In either case, it is a good idea to wrap the card in bubble wrap to add an additional layer of protection.

A

E

B

To my
Valentine

F

C

The Rose is pink,
The Violet blue,
My heart is warm,
With love for you

D

enlarge 200%

Sunbeam Boy (alternate)

The simpler version of "Sunbeam Boy" uses the center portion of the pop-up. The image was cut without intricate trimming and then elements were accented with coordinating glitter. The pop-up was layered on top of a paint chip sample, which features colors and names that describe this cherub: "sugared shortbread," "blonde beauty," and "sunbeam."

✪ ADHESIVES

- Acid-free adhesive dispenser
- Glitter adhesive
- Glue dot

✪ MATERIALS

- Button: yellow rose
- Cardstock: light blue, yellow
- Glitter: ultra-fine clear, dark teal, gold, light teal, pearl white, yellow
- Paint chip with 3 colors
- Ribbon and fiber

✪ TOOLS

- Border punch
- Copier
- Craft knife
- Cutting mat
- Fine tip (for glue bottle)
- Pencil
- Ruler
- Scissors: craft, micro-tip
- Scoring tool

✿ INSTRUCTIONS

1 Copy and cut out A and B paper elements
(page 65). Using craft knife, cut out small
areas in background.

2 Cut and fold both pieces of cardstock to create
6"-square side-fold cards using scoring tool. Trim
one side edge of each card with border punch.
Adhere cards together with acid-free adhesive
dispenser so yellow cardstock is on inside of card,
with the punched side on the right side. Blue
cardstock should be on outside with punched side
on front right side. *Note:* Layers are staggered so
that each layer shows from front of card.

3 With glitter adhesive, embellish boy element (A)
with glitter: gold and yellow on hair; light and
dark teal on flowers; and pearl white and clear
on birds.

4 Adhere paint chip onto front of card and then
boy paper element on top, at front of card.

5 Place ribbon and fiber around fold and tie at top,
leaving small tails. Add button with glue dot and
write sentiment inside card, if desired.

*Reversing the card's exterior colors, featuring
the same lacy border, extends the theme
to the interior of the design.*

Attaching Buttons
To attach buttons with shanks, remove the shank
with wire cutters and adhere onto the project
with thick glue dots. For a firmer hold,
consider using a hot glue gun.

Big Band Music

Original Card

The image for Big Band Music was printed onto a transparency to achieve an aged celluloid quality. It was then layered over white paper and held in place with heart brads. The urn is filled with paper hydrangeas and sprinkled with yellow and green glitter to accent the yellow of the transparency. The gold cardstock acts as both a card and an easel.

✿ ADHESIVES

- Acid-free adhesive dispenser
- Clear-drying craft glue
- Glitter adhesive

✿ MATERIALS

- Brads: red hearts (2 sizes)
- Cardstock: gold, white
- Chalk: deep blue
- Decorative paper: musical notes
- Glitter: ultra-fine pale green, yellow
- Paper flowers: blue
- Photo corners: black (4)
- Sentiment
- Transparency sheet

✿ TOOLS

- Copier
- Craft knife
- Cutting mat
- Pencil
- Ruler
- Scissors: craft, micro-tip
- Scoring tool

Music has charms to soothe a savage beast. – *William Congreve*

✿ INSTRUCTIONS

1 Copy and cut out paper elements (page 71). Using craft knife, cut out small areas in background.

2 Adhere back of card base (B) to underside of base (D) using acid-free adhesive dispenser.

3 Print flower paper element (A) onto transparency; adhere to slightly larger piece of white cardstock and chalk edges blue.

4 Using glitter adhesive, embellish flowers with pale green and yellow glitter; allow to dry. Glue paper flowers to flowers on top of urn (A).

5 To assemble card: Fold up bottom fifth of card using scoring tool. Adhere flower paper element (A) to center of card base with paper tabs (C).

6 Cut and fold gold cardstock to create 5"x7" side-fold card using scoring tool. Adhere musical notes paper and photo corners using acid-free adhesive dispenser.

7 Adhere pop-up to card with brads. Add three small brads along bottom base of card. Secure sentiment at top with small brad.

The greeting on the underside of the base is hidden when the card is displayed.

The pop-up is mounted on a pre-made card, which gives it a more sturdy foundation.

Experimenting with Paper

Copy centers offer a wide range of papers that can be used for reproducing the pop-up images. Experiment with different colors of cardstock and paper. Color-copying images onto transparencies creates an aged, celluloid-type look but be careful not to overuse it. Vellum only works in very limited amounts and tends to be too translucent to stand out from the underlying artwork.

A

B

To my Valentine

C

D

A Heartening Hello

The Heartening Hello project uses techniques including intricate cutting, glittering, and heat embossing. The coat-of-armor background, bird, and heart pieces were separated to produce a better view of each item when the card is displayed. A banner containing a definition of "hearten" is layered in front to lift the spirits of the recipient.

Original Card

✿ ADHESIVES

- Acid-free adhesive dispenser
- Clear-drying craft glue
- Glitter adhesive

✿ MATERIALS

- Dictionary definition
- Embossing inkpad: clear
- Embossing powder: gold
- Glitter: ultra-fine dark blue, gold, light blue, pink, red
- Leafing pen: gold
- Silk flowers: rose petals, rosebud

✿ TOOLS

- Copier
- Craft knife
- Cutting mat
- Fine tips (for glue bottles)
- Heat tool
- Scissors: craft, micro-tip
- Scoring tool

heart.en (här'tən) *v.t.* To give heart or courage to.

1 Copy and cut out paper elements (page 75). Using craft knife, cut out small areas in background.

2 Adhere back of card base (C) to underside of base (E) using acid-free adhesive dispenser.

3 Sprinkle gold embossing powder on gold areas and apply heat tool to emboss. Edge all cuts with gold leafing pen.

4 Using small amounts of glitter adhesive, embellish flowers, hearts, and girl's hair with glitter to match: red on hearts, gold on hair, and pink and blues on flowers.

5 To assemble card: Fold up bottom fourth of card using scoring tool. Glue bird paper element (A) to card using paper tab (D); glue girl paper element (B) in front of card using paper tab (D).

6 Glue silk petals to base of card to cover bare spots; glue rosebud to front of base.

7 Enlarge dictionary definition 130% on copier; trim ends into "V" cut. Glue definition across top of card.

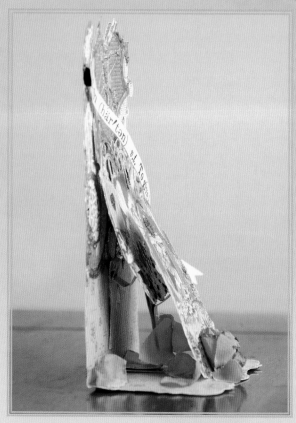

A scattering of pink silk rose petals helps disguise the paper tabs of the pop-up piece.

Heighten the Senses

Pop-up cards are very interactive and involve senses of sight and touch. Add a drop of rose or lavender essential oil for even more sensory appeal.

A

B

C

A token of Affection

D

E

enlarge 120%

Bouquet of Good Wishes

The original image for Bouquet of Good Wishes was enlarged to show the tiny words on the stem of each flower. The layered piece was attached to a gold embossed card to support the project's weight. A color photocopy of an autograph book page is tucked into the bottom of the card.

Original Card

✿ ADHESIVES

- Acid-free adhesive dispenser
- Glitter adhesive

✿ MATERIALS

- Cardstock: gold-embossed
- Glitter: ultra-fine dark blue, hunter green, light blue, pale yellow, and pink
- Inkpad: brown
- Lace
- Leafing pen: gold
- Old letter (optional)
- Paper towel

✿ TOOLS

- Copier
- Cosmetic sponge
- Craft knife
- Cutting mat
- Fine tip (for glue bottle)
- Pencil
- Ruler
- Scissors: craft, micro-tip

March 4th 1888

Emma L. Ritchie

Remember me when far away
If only half awake Remember
Me on your Wedding day
And send me a piece Of cake

1 Copy and cut out paper elements (page 79). Using craft knife, cut out small areas in background.

2 Paint edges of flower paper elements (A-G) with leafing pen, taking care to paint nooks to hide any rough spots.

3 With glitter adhesive and glitter, embellish fine lines on like colors of flowers to highlight. *Note:* Be sure to use light touches of glitter only; do not cover images with glitter.

4 Cut slits in visible lines below each art vignette; slide in a glittered, gilded flower. *Note:* Each vignette has a barely visible cut mark at the bottom of the scene. Some cuts are angled. Follow each line with a craft knife to cut a slit, which will open to hold the tab ends of the individual flowers.

5 Antique 6"-square piece of gold-embossed cardstock by wiping on brown ink with cosmetic sponge and then immediately wipe off most of stain with paper towel; allow to dry thoroughly.

6 Mount floral piece (H) onto gold-embossed cardstock folded into 3"x6" side-fold card. If desired, tuck in old letter or note that has been color copied or write new sentiments.

A color photocopy of a vintage note adds a touch of romance without endangering the original.

The side-fold card functions both as a place to write a note and as a frame for the bouquet.

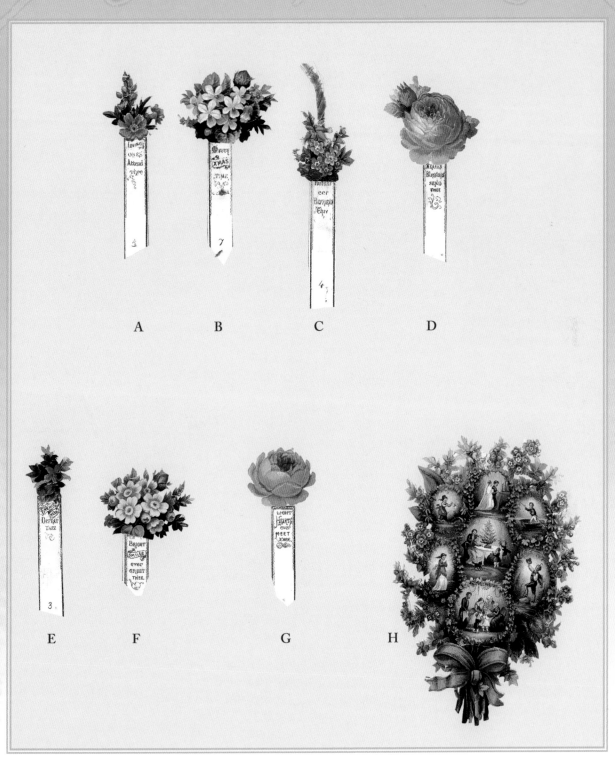

A   B   C   D

E   F   G   H

enlarge 140%

Valentine Greetings

Original Card

The various layers of Valentine Greetings sport vibrant red glitter, a tiny folded paper hat, and distressed paper pompoms. These whimsical touches enhance the impact of the card without making it too feminine—perfect for a special man in your life.

✿ ADHESIVES

- Acid-free adhesive dispenser
- Acid-free cellophane tape
- Fabric glue
- Foam dots
- Glitter adhesive

✿ MATERIALS

- Beads: red bugle
- Brads: gold (2)
- Cardstock: dark red
- Craft wire
- Glitter: ultra-fine blue, deep red, gold, red
- Inkpads: black, brown
- Paper: newspaper print, plain white
- Ribbon: brown silk
- Seed beads: red
- Sentiment

✿ TOOLS

- Border punch
- Computer and printer
- Copier
- Cosmetic sponge
- Craft knife
- Cutting mat
- Fine tips (for glue bottles)
- Piercing tool
- Scallop punch: circle
- Scissors: craft, micro-tip
- Wire cutters

1 Copy and cut out paper elements (page 83), copying two sets of Valentine Thoughts paper element (C) and big heart with arrow paper element from card base (E).

2 Layer duplicate elements with foam dots. Using glitter adhesive, embellish fine lines on roses, scrolls, and heart of card base (E) with deep red glitter; embellish arrow with gold glitter, drying between colors.

3 String bugle beads onto two lengths of wire. Adhere to base of card as pictured; secure at back with tape.

4 Glue two lengths of brown silk ribbon to top and bottom of Valentine Thoughts paper element (C) with fabric glue. Punch two scalloped circles from dark red cardstock. Crumple circles and then ink edges with cosmetic sponge and black and brown inkpads; crumple again to distress. Attach to Valentine Thoughts paper element with brads, using piercing tool to make pilot holes. *Note:* If desired, add dabs of brown ink on white areas.

5 Using glitter adhesive, embellish lines on angel draping (A) with blue glitter and sailor boy's heart (B) with red glitter.

The angel image was only lightly glittered to keep from overwhelming the project with glitter.

6 Fold newspaper hat to fit sailor boy and glue sentiment to hat; adhere hat onto sailor boy paper element (B) with acid-free adhesive dispenser.

7 To assemble card: Using acid-free adhesive dispenser, adhere Valentine Thoughts paper element (C) to card base (E). Attach angel (A) and sailor boy (B) to front of card using paper tabs (D).

Covering Up Flaws
Camouflage missing or damaged parts of a vintage card by adding new paper pieces to cover up the flawed portions.

A

B

E

C

VALENTINE
THOUGHTS

D

enlarge 185%

Eloise's Garden Party

The gardening pop-up of Eloise's Garden Party is attached to the front of a handmade pocket that contains a tag-shaped party invitation. Trimmed with decorative-edge scissors and accented with glitter, vellum, mulberry paper, brads, and a charm, the card is full of details.

Original Card

❀ ADHESIVES

- Acid-free adhesive dispenser
- Fabric glue
- Glitter adhesive
- Tacky double-sided tape

❀ MATERIALS

- Brads: jeweled (4)
- Cardstock: light green, tan
- Charm: garden-themed
- Glitter: ultra-fine clear, dark purple, dark rose, dark teal, hunter green, light green, light purple, light teal, medium purple
- Mulberry paper: purple
- Silk ribbon: green, purple
- Trim: green velvet (2 styles)
- Vellum

❀ TOOLS

- Computer and printer
- Copier
- Craft knife
- Cutting mat
- Fine tips (for glue bottles)
- Hole punch: mini
- Pencil
- Ruler
- Scissors: craft, decorative-edge scallop, micro-tip
- Scoring tool

✿ INSTRUCTIONS

1 Copy and cut out paper elements (page 87). Using craft knife, cut out small areas in background.

2 Adhere back of card base (B) to underside of base (D) with acid-free adhesive dispenser. Fold up bottom third of card base using scoring tool.

3 Using glitter adhesive and glitter, embellish paper elements (A, D): purples for tree flowers; dark rose on girl's dress; dark and light teal on background flowers; hunter green and light green on leaves between flowers; and clear glitter on birds and the backdrop.

4 Glue green velvet trim at bottom to form grass using fabric glue. With glitter adhesive and hunter green glitter, embellish boy's suit (A).

5 To assemble card: Attach boy and girl paper element (A) to card base with paper tab (C). Using fabric glue, embellish front of card base with coordinating velvet trim.

6 To create envelope: Cut 6"x12" piece of light green cardstock. Trim long edges with decorative-edge scissors. Fold up using scoring tool, short edge to short edge, matching scallops on

The more formal font on the tag suggests a serious occasion, while the larger font is a more light-hearted, casual font that complements the spirit of the invite.

sides. Punch holes in scallops. Layer with scalloped vellum at top and torn mulberry paper on front of envelope. Add brad at each corner to form pocket.

7 To create tag: Print text onto center of tan cardstock. Cut into tag shape that will fit in pocket easily. Trim hole with a scalloped oval cut from light green cardstock. Tie on ribbon and charm.

8 Attach glittered and trimmed pop-up to front of envelope with double-sided tape. Insert tag.

Experiment with Glitter

Use glitter to change trees or flower blossoms to fit a different color scheme. Blue blooms become purple when using translucent lavender glitter. Experiment with different colors and discover the wide range of combinations you can produce.

A

C

B

To my
Valentine

D

Love Boat

Original Card

The Love Boat project is an example of omitting an element because it overpowers the rest of the project. Removing the flowers from the original card allows the ship to move to the forefront. Pearls, gold rope trim, and a "borrowed" sentiment complete the card.

✿ ADHESIVES

- Acid-free adhesive dispenser
- Fabric glue
- Foam dots
- Glitter adhesive
- Glue dots

✿ MATERIALS

- Brad: blue rhinestone
- Embossing inkpad: clear
- Glitter: ultra-fine shades of blue, gold, pearl white, pink
- Inkpads: brown, clear
- Leafing pen: gold
- Pigment powder: pearl white
- Strands of mini pearls

✿ TOOLS

- Border punch
- Copier
- Cosmetic sponge
- Fine tips (for glue bottles)
- Paintbrush
- Scallop punch: circle
- Scissors: craft, micro-tip
- Scoring tool

✿ INSTRUCTIONS

1 Copy and cut out paper elements (page 91), copying two white sails (D).

2 Adhere back of card base (B) to underside of base (D) using acid-free adhesive dispenser. Fold up bottom third of card base using scoring tool.

3 Paint outer edges of base (D) with rope-type marks using gold leafing pen.

4 To embellish sail: Dab sail paper element (D) on clear inkpad; allow to dry. Dust with pigment powder and brush with paintbrush; repeat another 2-3 times, until surface is pearly. Hide glue square mark on original paper piece by dabbing extra pigment powder on mark. Dot glitter adhesive around heart; sprinkle on blue and gold glitter. Highlight top edge of sail with leafing pen.

5 Using glitter adhesive, embellish blue roses (D) sparingly with pearl white and blue glitter. Embellish shading on children and basket (A) using pink glitter. Add pearl white glitter to white parts of roses.

The small book, which was made with two copies of the original card base element, was wire-bound at a copy center and contains an inspiring quote.

6 Using fabric glue, adhere pearl strands to card base to mimic waves.

7 To assemble card: Cut out and attach sail to base with foam dots, one layer at bottom and one layer on top to make it bow outward. Attach children paper element (A) with paper tabs (C) and glue dots.

Strengthening Card Bases

For best results on projects with a considerable amount of embellishing, use heavy cardstock, preferably 110 lb. Simply adding glue and glitter creates more weight than might be expected.

A

B

To My Valentine.

C

D

enlarge 125%

Windmill Girl

The Windmill Girl is a multi-purpose greeting card that can be personalized with a valentine message or birthday greeting. The original card image was too small to accommodate the doll plate adorning the windmill so it was enlarged by 130%. The project is freestanding as in the original design but could be attached to the face of a card if desired.

Original Card

✿ ADHESIVES

- Acid-free adhesive dispenser
- Craft glue
- Foam dots
- Glitter adhesive
- Glue dots

✿ MATERIALS

- Die-cuts: blue flowers (13), decorative circle
- Glitter: ultra-fine dark blue, deep rose, light blue, pearl white, red
- Leafing pen: gold
- Rhinestones: light blue (13)
- Toothpicks: flat

✿ TOOLS

- Copier
- Fine tips (for glue bottles)
- Scissors: craft, micro-tip
- Scoring tool

To my Valentine
'Tis my delight to
bring you this
within its folds
you'll find a kiss.

✿ INSTRUCTIONS

1 Copy and cut out paper elements (page 95), creating two girl paper elements (A). *Note:* You will only need the heart from the second girl paper element.

2 Adhere back of card base (B) to underside of base (D) using acid-free adhesive dispenser. Fold up bottom third of card base using scoring tool.

3 Using glitter adhesive, embellish with glitter: bird on top of base light blue; flowers with light and dark blues; pink bow with deep rose; white on sleeves and lace ruffle at bottom of skirt with pearl white; and heart with red. Paint sides of paper elements and blades of windmill with leafing pen.

4 With glitter adhesive, embellish second heart with red glitter; adhere to girl paper element (A) with foam dot. Highlight with leafing pen as desired.

5 To assemble card: Attach girl paper element (A) to base (D) with paper tabs (C). Embellish flower die cuts with rhinestones and glue onto toothpicks, trimming bottom of toothpicks so "stems" are different lengths; leave four without stems. Allow to dry. Glue flowers and adhere circle die cut with foam dot to front of card.

The underside of the card base reveals a sentimental greeting.

Creating Extra Projects

Reduce images of simpler pop-ups to use as embellishments on envelopes, gifts, and note cards. Or, create a new project such as a garland using elements from existing designs.

A

D

B

With
loving Greeting.

C

To my Valentine.
'Tis my delight to
bring you this
within its folds
you'll find a kiss.

Baby Rose

The Baby Rose card presented the challenge of converting a religious pop-up to a more general theme for a wider range of uses. The halo was removed and replaced with a falling rosebud, the manger straw was layered with pink braid, and the baby was covered with a snippet of cream silk ribbon.

✿ ADHESIVES

- Acid-free adhesive dispenser
- Clear-drying craft glue
- Glitter adhesive

✿ MATERIALS

- Glitter: ultra-fine dark pink, dark teal, light pink, light teal, pale yellow, pearl white, rose
- Leafing pen: gold
- Ribbon: cream silk
- Silk flowers
- Trim: pink braid

✿ TOOLS

- Copier
- Craft knife
- Cutting mat
- Fabric glue
- Fine tips (for glue bottles)
- Scissors: craft, fabric, micro-tip
- Scoring tool

The bottom of the pop-up card folds up to reveal a pretty floral illustration.

1 Copy and cut out paper elements (page 99). Using craft knife, cut out small areas in background.

2 Adhere back of card base (G) to underside of base (H) using acid-free adhesive dispenser. Fold up bottom third of card base using scoring tool.

3 Paint all cut edges of paper elements with gold leafing pen.

4 Using glitter adhesive, embellish tiny amounts of paper elements (A-F) with glitter, changing colors to match the image; allow to dry between each color.

5 Cut halo off of baby element (B), leaving the straw. Lay pink trim along bottom row of manger and make pleats or loose ruffles. Adhere both ends of braid at back. Repeat in upper row with satin ribbon, drawing it closely around baby's neck. Glue on silk flowers as desired.

6 To assemble card: Adhere baby paper element (B) to back of card base (H) with paper tabs (I); adhere roses paper elements (E, F) to sides of card base with paper tabs (I); adhere floral swag paper element (A) at front of card with paper tabs (F).

Differences of Paper

Off-white or ivory cardstock can be especially beautiful because even the unprinted backs of the card will have a vintage look. Just remember that printing or copying the image onto colored cardstock or paper will alter the color of the image.

A

B

C

D

E

F

G

H

I

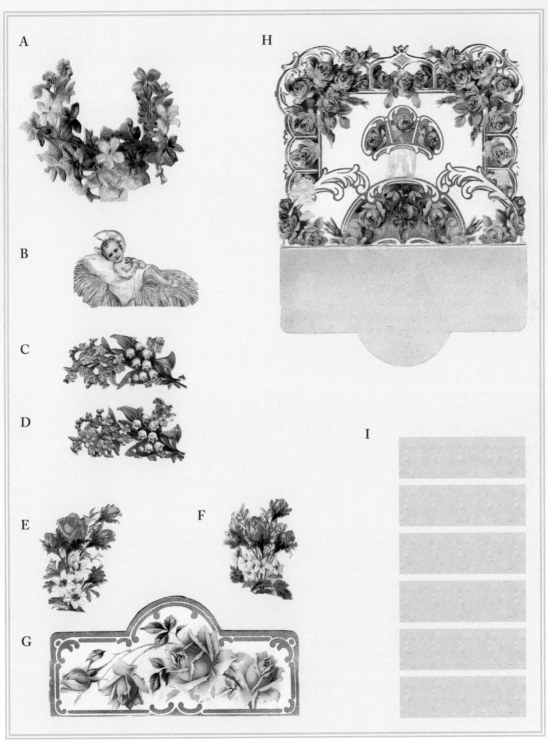

enlarge 145%

Love's Greeting

Original Card

The design of Love's Greeting showcases its elements using a sequence different from the original card. The large heart is embellished with flat silk flowers and a few strategically placed rosebuds. The greeting, accented with a silk cord and tassel, is now a part of the dimensional display.

✿ ADHESIVES

- Clear-drying craft glue
- Fabric glue
- Glitter adhesive
- Glue dots

✿ MATERIALS

- Acrylic paint: pearl white
- Decorative paper: desired color for base
- Glitter: ultra-fine clear, dark pink, dark teal, hunter green, light pink, light teal, white
- Paper flowers: forget-me-nots (2 shades of blue), rosebuds
- Pigment powder: pearl white
- Tassel: blue with cord

✿ TOOLS

- Copier
- Craft knife
- Cutting mat
- Fine tips (for glue bottles)
- Paintbrush
- Pencil
- Ruler
- Scissors: craft, decorative-edge, fabric, micro-tip

✿ INSTRUCTIONS

1 Copy and cut out paper elements (page 103). Using craft knife, cut out small areas in background.

2 Glue forget-me-not flowers onto large heart (D). Using glitter adhesive, embellish paper elements with glitter: dark teal on center portion of darkest flowers; light teal glitter on center of lightest flowers; white glitter on lilies of the valley and dove; dark and light pinks on small portions of each rose; and hunter green on tips of leaves. *Note:* When covering heart with flowers, leave small gaps for adhering paper elements.

3 Glue rosebuds on front of pink heart (B). Paint bird with acrylic paint, then sprinkle on pigment powder and dust with paintbrush; allow to dry. Apply small amounts of glue and then sprinkle on clear glitter. *Note:* Do not reapply pearl powder over areas that already have glitter; it looks best if the bird is highlighted, not coated, with glitter.

4 To assemble card: Cut 8" circular base with decorative-edge scissors. Attach base (D) with paper tab (E); glue hearts paper element (B) to front of base with paper tab (E), then glue dove paper element (A) with paper tab (E). Secure sentiment paper element (C) with glue dots so that it shows when card is upright.

5 Adhere tassel to sentiment paper element (C) using fabric glue. Glue to circular base.

The embellished greeting portion of the card was used to incorporate the base into the overall display.

Layering With Like Items

For a more cohesive design, mimic the printed image by layering similar paper flowers or embellishing details with coordinating glitter colors. This will increase the image's impact.

A

D

B

C

E

enlarge 115%

Valentine Keeper

Original Card

While most illustrations of Victorian children depict miniature adults, the Valentine Keeper card's girl in the simple dress actually looks like a child. The clothing, hair, and elongated art background hint at the future. As a decorative valentine or a paper doll, this card truly is a keeper.

✿ ADHESIVES

- Clear-drying craft glue
- Foam dots
- Glitter adhesive
- Tacky double-sided tape

✿ MATERIALS

- Embossing inkpad: clear
- Embossing powder: clear
- Glitter: ultra-fine dark blue, gold, light blue, red
- Leafing pen: gold
- Pigment powder: gold
- Rhinestones: heart-shaped
- Ribbon with sentiment
- Sequins: heart-shaped

✿ TOOLS

- Copier
- Cosmetic sponge
- Craft knife
- Craft tweezers
- Cutting mat
- Fine tips (for glue bottles)
- Heat tool
- Paintbrush
- Scissors: craft, micro-tip, scallop-edge

❋ INSTRUCTIONS

1 Copy and cut out two sets of paper elements (page 107). *Note:* One set is for layering elements.

2 Set 1: Cut out all details. Using craft knife, cut out small areas in background. Set 2: Cut out doll and large hearts at girl's feet (A).

3 Adhere back of base (B) to underside of base (D) with double-sided tape.

4 Rub Set 1 and pieces from Set 2 with inkpad using cosmetic sponge and then coat entire surface with embossing powder; apply heat tool to emboss, using craft tweezers and following all safety precautions. Repeat 2-3 times, allowing to cool between each application. Flatten between applications to prevent curling.

5 Hold papers in hands and bend in all directions to gently crack surface. *Note:* A small snap sound will be heard.

6 Apply pigment powder with paintbrush and rub into cracks. *Note:* There is no medium required for this step as the coated surface has a bit of residual tackiness that has enough to grab pigment powder; the gold will randomly adhere to the entire surface.

Another version of the Valentine Keeper card, this pop-up uses only the girl element without the background.

7 Glue sequins and rhinestones onto heart images. Using glitter adhesive, embellish with glitter: gold on girl's hair; blues on flowers around her head; and red on backdrop.

8 Using cut pieces of foam dots, adhere doll and two hearts at girl's feet. Embellish with glitter as desired.

9 Attach girl (A) to background (D) with paper tab (C). Glue ribbon sentiment onto base. Embellish with heart sequin.

Adequate Lighting

When working with finely detailed projects, good lighting is essential for comfortable cutting and embellishing. Be sure you have a good combination of natural and task lighting to prevent eyestrain and tense muscles.

A

D

B

My Valentine

WHENEVER YOU COME INTO MIND
I HAVE TO SEND A WISH OR TWO,
AND SO, IN SUMMING UP, I FIND
I THINK-O, SUCH A LOT OF YOU.

Printed in Germany

C

enlarge 115%

Jeweled Heart

The Jeweled Heart card uses clear embossing powder to mimic an enamel or painted porcelain finish as well as to add strength and stiffness for lifting the layers. Adhesive jewels in sapphire blue and clear give a bit of sparkle, while a delicate lace border adds detail.

Original Card

✿ ADHESIVES

- Clear-drying craft glue
- Fabric glue
- Foam dots
- Glitter adhesive

✿ MATERIALS

- Embossing inkpad: clear
- Embossing powder: clear, gold
- Glitter: ultra-fine deep pink, gold, light blue, pearl white
- Lace: cream
- Leafing pen: gold
- Paper hinge stickers, purchased or homemade
- Rhinestone jewel stickers: blue, clear

✿ TOOLS

- Copier
- Craft knife
- Cutting mat
- Fine tip (for glue bottles)
- Heat tool
- Paintbrush
- Scissors: fabric, micro-tip

✿ INSTRUCTIONS

1 Copy and cut out paper elements (page 111), copying four sets of elements (A-C). Using craft knife, cut out small areas in background.

2 To embellish heart base: Sprinkle base (C) with clear powder and then apply heat tool to emboss. Emboss with gold embossing powder as accents, including around outer border. Repeat 2-3 times for each paper element, allowing to cool between each application. Adhere blue and clear jewels around seashells and as desired. Match sizes and colors of jewels on both sides of heart.

3 Attach heart base (C) to bottom text layer (D) with two paper hinge stickers glued at top. Adhere jewels on hinges. Glue lace to reverse side of card with fabric glue.

4 To embellish harp layer: Emboss element (A) several times, allowing to cool between each application. Highlight with gold leafing pen. Cut extra flowers from harp paper elements and paint edges with leafing pen. Using glitter adhesive, embellish flowers with deep pink glitter; add gold glitter to flower centers. Adhere clear jewels to top of harp and blue jewels to left and right top. Glitter fairy cutout and paint with leafing pen. Adhere cutouts to harp with

The interior of the card was accented with a vintage picture and a sentiment.

foam dots. Adhere harp to big heart (C) with foam dots.

5 To embellish top layer: Emboss lace frame (B) with clear powder. With adhesive glue and glitter, embellish leaf and flowers. Adhere jewels to center of flowers. Using multiple stacks of foam dots, adhere glittered flowers and cherub to top layer. Adhere top layer to harp layer with foam dots placed strategically so they don't show through lacy layer. Adhere to heart base (C) with foam dots.

Achieving a Porcelain Effect
Clear embossing powders applied several times all over the card lend a porcelain quality to simple papers.

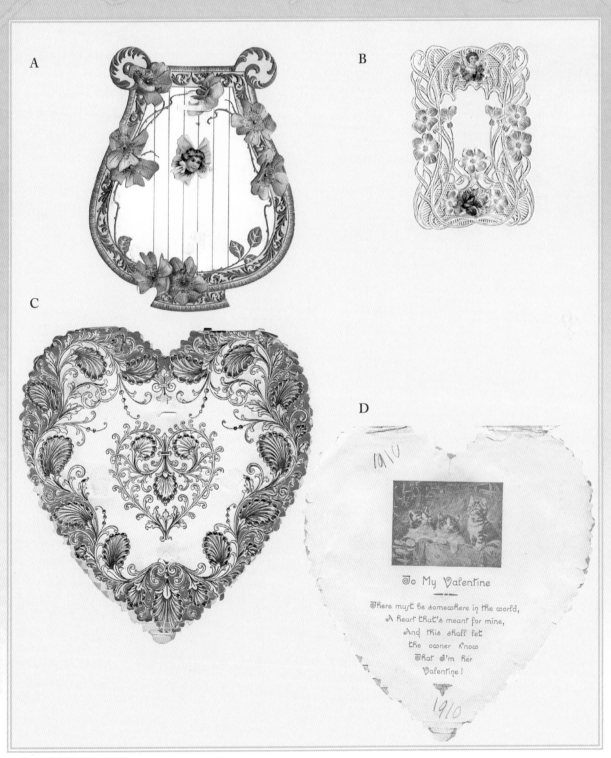

A

B

C

D

To My Valentine

There must be somewhere in the world,
A heart that's meant for mine,
And this shall let
the owner know
That I'm her
Valentine!

1910

1910

enlarge 250%

Happy Birthday Queen

Original Card

The front panel of the Happy Birthday Queen card lifts to reveal two inner pages: the vintage text page and an easel layer with the word "play." Collage-style embellishments, charms, and a velvet ribbon complement the bright poppies.

✪ ADHESIVES

- Clear-drying craft glue
- Foam dots
- Glitter adhesive
- Glue dots

✪ MATERIALS

- Beads: gold bugle
- Birthday foil crown (with headband removed)
- Candles: gold
- Chalk
- Charm: crown
- Clock face
- Computer-printed or rubber-stamped message
- Decorative paper: yellow-and-white polka dot
- Doilies: white
- Foil sticker: Happy Birthday
- Glitter: ultra-fine gold, light orange, rust; vintage glass gold
- Inkpad: black
- Leafing pen: gold
- Paper leaves and hinges
- Ribbon: velvet

✪ TOOLS

- Copier
- Craft knife
- Cutting mat
- Fine tips (for glue bottles)
- Sandpaper
- Scissors: fabric, micro-tip, scallop-edge

1   Copy and cut out two sets of paper elements
    (page 115). Using craft knife, cut out small areas
    in background.

2   Cut decorative paper to mirror base of card (A),
    making it 1" wider on each side and 3" taller.
    Add polka dot easel to back and stamp "play" on
    it. *Note:* This card lies flat unless it is leaned up
    against something. To make an easel, fold and
    attach a piece of cardstock to the back.

3   Glue lace doily pieces to underside of text,
    matching edges. Use paper hinges to attach girl
    page (A) on top of text page (C). Using glue
    dots, adhere extra copies of gold leafed flowers,
    candles, crown on girl's head, caption, clock, and
    velvet ribbon. Highlight with gold leafing pen.
    Glitter flowers in matching colors and adhere
    with stacks of foam dots. Adhere girl page and
    its hinged partner to decorative paper. Fill in top
    border area with doilies and extra poppies and
    then glue paper leaves under stacks of poppies.

4   Remove band from crown. Sand letters on crown
    lightly to prepare surface for glue. Apply glit-
    ter adhesive and cover with 2-3 coats of vintage
    glass glitter; allow to dry.

*The card interior features a vintage image
and text layered over a lace doily.*

5   Cut out two faces/heart image and pansy image
    from unused doily piece (B). Layer each with
    foam dot and adhere to front of card on left and
    right sides of heart, holding Birthday Queen im-
    age in place. Discard remainder of doily image.
    Add foil sticker to inside of card.

Test the Design

Test the design of the card by assembling the
undecorated pieces using repositionable
adhesive. This way, you can be sure all the
parts are accounted for and everything works
smoothly. Once the assembly is complete, the
entire card can be taken apart. Reassemble the
finished card using a strong permanent adhesive.

A

C

B

FOR MY VALENTINE

I've waited for a long, long time,
For a chance to say,
"Oh! will you be MY VALENTINE
To-day and everyday?"

enlarge 215%

Game of Love

Original Card

The Game of Love is adhered onto a top-folding card to provide support and a display surface. Several of the diamonds on the background paper have been glittered, creating a strong visual impact. Dollhouse miniatures and game piece letters spell out "hugs and kisses."

✿ ADHESIVES

- Acid-free adhesive dispenser
- Clear-drying craft glue
- Fabric glue
- Foam dots
- Glitter adhesive

✿ MATERIALS

- Beaded tassel: red
- Brads: pewter (2)
- Cardstock: red
- Decorative paper: diamond, hearts
- Embellishments: dollhouse dart board with feather dart, domino, game pieces, letter tags, mini clothespins, mini playing cards
- Glitter: chunky black, red; ultra-fine red, white
- Inkpad: black
- Paper: white
- Silk roses: mini red
- Trim: zigzag

✿ TOOLS

- Computer and printer
- Copier
- Cosmetic sponge
- Craft knife
- Cutting mat
- Fine tips (for glue bottles)
- Paintbrush
- Paper punch: mini heart
- Pencil
- Piercing tool
- Ruler
- Scissors: craft, micro-tip, scallop-edge
- Scoring tool

1 Copy and cut out paper elements (page 119). Using craft knife, cut out small areas in background.

2 Adhere back of card base (C) to underside of base (D) using acid-free adhesive dispenser. Fold up bottom third of card base using scoring tool.

3 To make background: Cut and fold red cardstock to create 8"x5" top-fold card using scoring tool. Using glitter adhesive, embellish diamond decorative paper as shown with chunky red and black glitter, one color at a time; allow to dry for a day.

4 Using glitter adhesive, embellish roses on paper element (A) with ultra-fine red glitter and angel wings with white glitter; adhere to front of card base (D) with paper tab (B). Glue hearts decorative paper and game letters to floor of card base.

5 Adhere diamond paper to front left of card with acid-free adhesive dispenser. Pierce two holes at left and insert brads, looping tassel before closing prongs.

6 Attach zigzag trim along bottom edge with fabric glue.

7 Attach pop-up to right side of diamond card with acid-free adhesive tape.

8 At left of card, glue on game pieces and letters. Punch mini-heart for center of dartboard; glue on and then add darts. Attach playing cards with clothespins to right side of card. *Note:* Try to use a king and queen of hearts or king of hearts and queen of diamonds.

9 Print title on white paper using computer. With cosmetic sponge and black inkpad, wipe edges with ink; glue onto red cardstock and adhere to card with foam dots.

Handling Chunky Glitter

Though they are beautiful to look at, chunky glitters are truly glass and can cut hands and fingers with casual handling. When using chunky glitter, be very careful and keep away from children. It is advisable to stick to non-glass glitters for cards or other projects that will be touched a great deal.

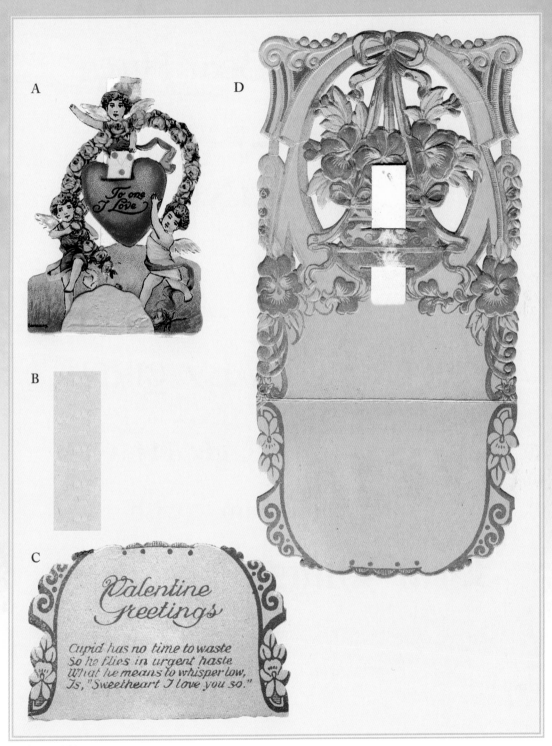

A

B

C

Valentine Greetings

Cupid has no time to waste
So he flies in urgent haste
What he means to whisper low,
Is, "Sweetheart I love you so."

D

Bear Hugs

PUT ON YOUR THINKING CAP

Bear Hugs

WELCOME BABY GIRL!

BEAR HUGS

hope   dream   wish

Bear Hugs

A SWEET BABY GIRL
TO LOVE

Bear Hugs

Sentiments to Inspire

Welcome Sweet Baby!

THINKING OF YOU

To my beloved valentine-

To My Beloved Valentine

Thinking of You

Thinking of You

Sentiments to Inspire

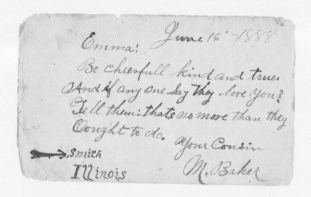

Emma! June 16 1888

Be cheerfull kind and true.
And if any one say they love you?
Tell them: thats no more than they
Ought to do.   Your Cousin

→ Smith   M. Baker
Illinois

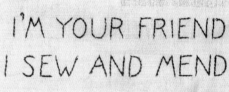

I'M YOUR FRIEND
I SEW AND MEND

True blue.   True Blue.

Merci.

Welcome Baby!

Merci.

congratulations graduate.

congratulations Sarah.

Sentiments to Inspire

And they lived happily ever after.

PUT ON YOUR THINKING CAP

And they lived happily ever after,

Sail away with me, Valentine

And they lived happily ever after.

And they lived happily ever after

And they lived happily ever after.

WELCOME BABY BOY!

And they lived happily ever after.

Acknowledgments

⭐ BOOK EDITOR

Catherine Risling

⭐ COPY EDITOR

Lisa Anderson

⭐ PROJECT DESIGNER

Marian Ballog

⭐ COPY CONTRIBUTORS

Marian Ballog
Lecia Monsen

⭐ PHOTOGRAPHER

Zachary Williams
Williams Visual
Ogden, UT

⭐ PHOTO STYLIST

Annie Hampton

⭐ BOOK DESIGNER

Dori Dixon
D3 Grafx, Inc.
Lake Elsinore, CA

Metric Equivalency Charts

inches to millimeters and centimeters

inches	mm	cm
1/8	3	0.3
1/4	6	0.6
1/2	13	1.3
5/8	16	1.6
3/4	19	1.9
7/8	22	2.2
1	25	2.5
1 1/4	32	3.2
1 1/2	38	3.8
1 3/4	44	4.4
2	51	5.1
2 1/2	64	6.4
3	76	7.6
3 1/2	89	8.9
4	102	10.2
4 1/2	114	11.4
5	127	12.7
6	152	15.2
7	178	17.8
8	203	20.3

inches	cm
9	22.9
10	25.4
12	30.5
13	33.0
14	35.6
15	38.1
16	40.6
17	43.2
18	45.7
19	48.3
20	50.8
21	53.3
22	55.9
23	58.4
24	61.0
25	63.5
26	66.0
27	68.6
28	71.1
29	73.7

inches	cm
30	76.2
31	78.7
33	83.8
34	86.4
35	88.9
36	91.4
37	94.0
38	96.5
39	99.0
40	101.6
41	104.1
42	106.7
43	109.2
44	111.8
45	114.3
46	116.8
47	119.4
48	121.9
49	124.5
50	127.0

yards to meters

yards	meters	yards	meters	yards	meters	yards	meters	yards	meters
1/8	0.11	2 1/8	0.11	4 1/8	3.77	6 1/8	5.6	8 1/8	7.43
1/4	0.23	2 1/4	0.23	4 1/4	3.89	6 1/4	5.72	8 1/4	7.54
3/8	0.34	2 3/8	0.34	4 3/8	4.0	6 3/8	5.83	8 3/8	7.66
1/2	0.46	2 1/2	0.46	4 1/2	4.11	6 1/2	5.94	8 1/2	7.77
5/8	0.57	2 5/8	0.57	4 5/8	4.23	6 5/8	6.06	8 5/8	7.89
3/4	0.69	2 3/4	0.69	4 3/4	4.34	6 3/4	6.17	8 3/4	8.00
7/8	0.80	2 7/8	0.80	4 7/8	4.46	6 7/8	6.29	8 7/8	8.12
1	0.91	3	0.91	5	4.57	7	6.40	9	8.23
1 1/8	1.03	3 1/8	1.03	5 1/8	4.69	7 1/8	6.52	9 1/8	8.34
1 1/4	1.14	3 1/4	1.14	5 1/4	4.80	7 1/4	6.63	9 1/4	8.46
1 3/8	1.26	3 3/8	1.26	5 3/8	4.91	7 3/8	6.74	9 3/8	8.57
1 1/2	1.37	3 1/2	1.37	5 1/2	5.03	7 1/2	6.86	9 1/2	8.69
1 5/8	1.49	3 5/8	1.49	5 5/8	5.14	7 5/8	6.97	9 5/8	8.80
1 3/4	1.60	3 3/4	1.60	5 3/4	5.26	7 3/4	7.09	9 3/4	8.92
1 7/8	1.71	3 7/8	1.71	5 7/8	5.37	7 7/8	7.20	9 7/8	9.03
2	1.83	4	1.83	6	5.49	8	7.32	10	9.14

Index

Index